Depression

Practical & Natural Approaches You Can Use To Cure Depression In The Moment & Long Term

Jane Aniston

Introduction

We all have days where it feels like nothing in life seems to be going right. Whether it's typical life struggles, setbacks, disappointments, losses or sometimes just minor annoyances that cause us inconvenience, they cast a gloomy cloud over us that makes us feel sad and down. When we are going through rough patches in life, we often use the word "depressed" to describe the sinking feeling which is engulfing us.

Normally, once the ordeal is over, the feeling of doom and gloom will pass, and our outlook will improve. But what if, rather than our mood improving after these temporary setbacks, the gloomy feelings never seem to leave. What if these feelings keep on recurring, even when there is no obvious reason to feel sad? Depression is no longer just a normal state when it begins to adversely affect the way one thinks, feels and acts on a daily basis. Persistent feelings of sadness, hopelessness and emptiness are signs that one could be suffering from clinical depression – a mood disorder that can lead to a whole host of emotional and physical problems. Perhaps the most worrying consequence of clinical depression is that, if left untreated, it can lead to an individual having suicidal thoughts and in the worst cases even acting on them.

Fortunately, with knowledge and consistent effort, depression – whether clinical or not – can be managed and overcome. In this book we will look at depression from a medical standpoint, then move on to cover long-term solutions to prevent depression wrecking havoc on your life. Finally we'll cover a whole host of quick fixes that can be used in the moment to beat the blues.

By arming yourself with the knowledge and tools needed to break free from depressive thoughts, you will be able to adopt a more positive outlook, which in turn will result in a happier reality. No one should suffer from depression in silence.

Table of contents

Chapter 1

It's Not Just a Bad Day

Unlike ordinary sadness and grief, depression can develop into a form of mood disorder that causes a persistent feeling of despair, emptiness and unhappiness. This condition is known as clinical depression or major depressive disorder, and is a completely different and more dangerous kind of depression. It has a negative effect on a person's emotions, thoughts and behavior, making it a struggle for them to function normally, and feel joyful in their day-to-day life.

People who suffer from clinical depression often feel as if life is not worth living. Not all clinically depressed individuals experience immense sadness, though. Some may feel apathetic, angry, aggressive, restless and worthless. What separates a normal bout of feeling down from the more severe is that the negative emotions one feels are intense and relentless, with little to no rest bite. Furthermore, the feelings that plague depression sufferers can manifest as physical illnesses.

Are You Depressed?

Depression may occur only once during a person's lifetime, or one may experience multiple episodes of the condition. Identifying the signs and symptoms of depression can be tricky, mainly because they are often so severe and impactful on one's life. Moreover, depression varies from person to person in terms of severity. Symptoms experienced depend on one's age, gender, overall health and life circumstances. It should also be taken into account that many depression symptoms could well be part of life's normal lows, and not related to a mental condition.

The following is a list of common emotional and physiological symptoms of depression. The more of these symptoms a person has and the stronger and more frequent they are, the more likely one is dealing with depression. A sure sign of a problem is when the symptoms interfere with your regular daily routine and do not seem to abate, even when there are no obvious external causes for them.

- Feeling sad, helpless, hopeless, empty and having an overall bleak outlook that nothing can improve your situation

- Loss of interest in daily activities, socializing and things you used to enjoy

- Unusually short tempered, with frequent outbursts of tearfulness, anger, irritability or frustration, and even violent behavior

- Sleep troubles, including insomnia, radical change in sleeping habits and oversleeping

- Feeling anxious, agitated and restless for no rational reason

- Changes in appetite and body weight, either a significant reduce in appetite that cases weight loss, or an increase in food cravings that lead to weight gain

- Feeling low in energy. Sluggishness and fatigue to the point that simple tasks take extra effort to complete

- Difficulty thinking, concentrating, making decisions and remembering things, making tasks that were previously easy feel daunting

- Slowed response to speech and weakened reflexes

- Feeling worthless, self-loathing, guilt. Blaming oneself for things in the past that are not of your fault

- Uncontrollable negative thoughts that will not go away

- Engaging in reckless and risky escapist behavior, including substance abuse, excessive alcohol consumption, compulsive gambling, dangerous sports, reckless driving and frequent casual sex

- Unexplained physical ailments, such as headaches, back pain, muscle aches and stomach pain

- Frequent thoughts of self-harm, suicide and death

Chapter 2

What's Making You Depressed & Are You At Risk?

Depression is a complex mental disorder, and as with most conditions of this kind, it is tricky to pinpoint an exact cause. Most likely, there are various factors involved that causes one to be abnormally depressed. The following are commonly believed to be factors in the onset of depression:

- **Biological differences.** Research has found that people with clinical depression appear to have physical differences in their brains. For instance, part of the brain vital for storing memory, known as the hippocampus, appears to be smaller in the brains of those who have a history of depression than in those who do not. A smaller hippocampus means fewer receptors for the neurotransmitter serotonin, which is one of the brain chemicals that allow for communication across circuits connecting different regions of the brain. However, the significance of differences in brain structure as a cause of depression is still uncertain. Neither is it fully understood what really causes those changes.

- **Brain chemistry.** Naturally occurring brain chemical, known as neurotransmitters, are responsible for communicating information throughout the brain and body. Though nothing has been proven conclusively, there are researches suggesting that changes in the function and effect of neurotransmitters involved in maintaining mood stability may play a part in depression.

- **Hormonal imbalance.** Hormone changes due to pregnancy, giving birth, thyroid problems and a number of other constitutions may cause or trigger depression.

- **Family medical history.** Depression appears to be more common among people who have blood relatives with the condition, leading experts to believe that it could be a genetically inherited trait. Like with most factors believed to have caused depression, evidence in this area is still inconclusive.

- **Lifestyle and experiences.** Prolonged and poorly managed stress, traumatic experiences, physical and emotional abuse, high alcohol consumption and suffering from chronic illnesses are factors which can contribute to depression.

With an understanding of the causes of depression, it is also worth recognizing the factors that could increase a person's risk of developing this mental condition, so that measures can be taken to manage one's lifestyle and emotions before depression escalates. Depression can happen to anyone at any age, although it commonly begins in the teens, 20s or

30s. Generally, more women are diagnosed with depression than men, although this does not necessarily mean women are at higher risk; it could just be that women are more likely to seek medical attention than men.

These are the risk factors that seem to contribute to the development or triggering of depression:

- Having certain personality traits, such as low self-esteem, being overly self-critical, being too sensitive to criticism or being generally pessimistic

- Experiencing a traumatic or stressful event, such as physical, emotional or sexual abuse, the death or loss of a loved one, a difficult relationship, marital problems or financial troubles

- Having a traumatic experience during childhood or depression that started in the teenage years

- Having blood relatives with a history of depression or other mental illnesses, such as bipolar disorder, anxiety disorder, alcoholism or suicidal tendencies

- Being homosexual or transgendered in an unsupportive environment that subjects one to ridicule or bullying

- Having a history of other mental health conditions, such as anxiety disorder, eating disorders or post-traumatic stress disorder

- Abuse of alcohol or drugs

- Suffering from serious long-term illnesses, such as cancer, stroke, heart condition or chronic pain

- Temporary or prolonged use of certain medications, such as high blood pressure and sleep medications, could cause depression as a side-effect

- Feeling isolated, lonely and lack of social support during times of hardship and distress

Chapter 3

Never Leave Depression Alone

Feeling sad and down may be just a phase. However, clinical depression is a serious mental condition not to be taken lightly. Left untreated, depression can lead to a host of emotional, behavioral and physical health issues, wreaking havoc in many aspects of a person's life. Among the possible complications of severe depression are:

- Excess weight gain and obesity, which greatly heightens the risks of cancer, heart diseases and diabetes

- Drastic weight loss and developing an eating disorder

- Development of chronic pain and physical illnesses

- Alcohol and substance abuse with the risk of death from drug interactions and overdose

- Anti-social behavior

- Family, marital and other relationship difficulties

- Poor performance at work or school

- Self-harm and mutilation

- Worsening of other medical conditions, possibly even resulting in premature death

Of the complications that could result from depression, perhaps the most worrying of all is that the condition is a major risk factor for suicide. Overwhelming feelings of despair, hopelessness, and unworthiness can make depression sufferers feel like death is the only way out of their misery. If you or anyone you know suffers from depression, it is important that suicidal thoughts and behaviors be taken seriously. Learn to spot the following warning signs:

- Talking about killing or harming oneself

- Expressing strong feelings of hopelessness and being trapped

- Showing an unusual preoccupation with death

- Behaving recklessly without regards for one's safety, such as speeding, passing through red lights, using drugs and drinking copious amounts of alcohol

- Uncharacteristically calling or visiting people to say goodbye

- A preoccupation with getting affairs in order, like giving away prize possessions, having a will written and tying up loose ends

- Making remarks like "Everyone would be better off without me" or "I want out of this life"

- A sudden switch from being extremely depressed to being calm and happy

It is crucial to understand that people who are going through severe depression do not suddenly snap out of it, or eventually get over it. They will require some sort of help or long-term treatment. On a brighter note, there are many ways to combat depression. Methods to do so include making lifestyle changes, adopting daily habits to keep negative thoughts at bay, and in very severe cases, medication and therapy administered by a qualified mental healthcare specialist may be called for.

Chapter 4

A Practical Guide to Managing Emotions and Overcoming Depression - Part 1: *Physical Changes*

The first step to conquering depression is to understand the underlying cause. Only then can further steps be taken to healthily and safely tackle the root cause of unhappiness which is being experienced. There are plenty of practical methods one can use in order to overcome depression without resorting to psychotherapy and medication. For instance, if you are depressed about gaining weight, the sensible solution is to practice self-acceptance and take up an exercise program to help with weight management, rather than taking antidepressant medications. If you moved to a new neighborhood and feel lonely, getting involved with the community and making friends is a preferred option to therapy.

The information provided here is NOT intended as a substitute for professional medical attention. It is meant to help depression-prone individuals remedy their condition by changing the situations that are causing them to be feel depressed, and assist them in making long-term beneficial lifestyle changes. Anyone can adopt these methods; either as a supplement to clinical treatment, or just to improve overall outlook.

As discussed, the causes and symptoms of depression are different for each sufferer, and so it follows, so are the ways that will make them feel better. You do not have to follow all of the points outlined here. The methods listed are compiled for their proven effectiveness, and presented in a straightforward easy-to-follow manner. Also bear in mind that there is no one way to treat depression; the best approach often involves a combination of lifestyle changes, emotional management, social support and professional medical help.

Exercise, Exercise, Exercise!

Nothing makes a more effective antidepressant than to stop moping and get moving. It has been consistently proven in numerous studies that regular exercise – in fact, any form of physical activity – triggers the release of feel-good brain chemicals like endorphins. You are almost certain to feel an overall sense of well-being, sleep better at night and experience an improved mood.

If you have never been a regular exerciser before, try starting small and build up a habit. Take a stroll around the block in the morning, walk the dog, tend to your garden or pop in an exercise video and follow along. Start off by allocating two days a week for 15 to

30 minutes of exercise. Once you get into the habit of allocating time for exercising, gradually increase the duration and frequency until you are exercising four to six days a week.

When you have incorporated exercise into your regular routine, you may want to think about taking things further, such as joining a health club or taking up a sport of your choice. It does not matter what your choice of activity is or how intense it is; what matters is that you get moving regularly while doing something you enjoy. After all, if you don't enjoy an activity, it is likely that you won't continue with it long term. For example, if you do not enjoy jogging, opt for something else that you will look forward to, like golfing, swimming or cardio dancing.

It will also be helpful to have a workout buddy; an individual or a circle of friends who enjoy the same activities whom you can count on for support and motivation when it gets tough to stay on track. Moreover, staying connected with others is crucial for overcoming the exhaustions and isolation that could trigger depression.

Eat Healthy for the Mind and Body

There is no specific diet that works for depression, but a healthy and clean diet should be part of your overall treatment plan. This is because there is an undeniable connection between mind and body. Optimal physical health gives you the energy to participate in the activities you enjoy, which in turn contributes to overall emotional health. A sound diet plan should be built around adequate intake of nutrient-rich fruits, vegetables and whole grains.

There have been studies that suggest incorporating omega-3 fatty acids and vitamin B12 – especially for those who are deficient in these nutrients – may help ease mood changes that can contribute to depression. Not only that, omega-3 is shown to alleviate certain depression symptoms, such as sleep disorders, anxiety, and moodiness, in addition to lowering "bad cholesterol" and improving heart health.

Foods rich in omega-3 include fish such as salmon, tuna and mackerel. Alternatively, the fatty acid is also present in plant sources like flaxseed, walnuts, soybeans, and dark green vegetables. For your dose of B12, add more seafood and low-fat dairy products to your regular diet, or go for vegetarian sources like fortified cereals. Both nutrients are also commonly found in the form of supplement tablets, although obtaining them from natural sources is always preferred.

Reduce Caffeine and Avoid Alcohol

Thinking about reaching for that third cup of coffee for the day? While moderate amounts of caffeinated beverages are shown to have some health benefits (including assisting with memory), exceeding the daily recommended dose of two cups does more harm than good. There is no definitive link between caffeinated drinks and depression. However, too much caffeine can make you nervous and jittery, which may trigger anxiety or insomnia – both conditions known to accompany depression. Cutting back on caffeine intake may help lower the risk of depression by helping you relax and sleep better.

Although caffeinated beverages have some merit, alcoholic drinks have none whatsoever. It is a common mistake for people who feel depressed to use alcohol as a source of relief. In truth, alcohol does more harm than good. Firstly, alcohol is "empty calories", (meaning consuming it will add to your caloric count), providing no nutritional value to the body. Thus, alcohol contains no essential nutrients and eliminating it from your diet will not deprive you of any health benefits. Secondly, alcohol-induced sleep does not allow for the quality sleep necessary for the body to rest and rejuvenate.

If you suffer from depression, habitual alcohol consumption will only prolong and worsen your misery. Plus, if you are already taking medication for depression, alcohol can interfere with these antidepressants.

Make Quality Sleep a Priority

When someone shows up in the morning grouchy and moody, we often say he or she must have woken up on the wrong side of the bed. Well, there is a dose of truth to that expression. There is a strong connection between sleep and a stable mood.

Adequate sleep, along with exercise and a good diet, is a vital component for overall well-being. The effects of quality sleep are direct; you will have greater mental clarity and emotional balance, enhanced creativity, better productivity and more physical vitality. The typical adult needs seven to eight hours of restful sleep each night for the mind and body to fully rest and rejuvenate. Lack of sleep causes irritability, stress, and anxiety. Even short-term sleep deprivation can significantly affect one's quality of life.

Poor sleep can be both a cause and symptom of depression. On one hand, lack of sleep adversely affects mood. On another, depression interferes with sleep, causing the sufferer to sleep too much, or to have difficulty falling and staying asleep. Regardless of your situation, make an effort to cultivate good sleeping habits. Here are some key pointers to help you do so:

- Learn when to call it a day; when to stop any work you're doing, turn off the TV and make preparations to retire for the night.

- Go to bed and get up at around the same time every day. By keep a consistent sleep schedule, you are conditioning your mind and body to maintain a cycle of sleepiness and wakefulness.

- Go to sleep at night; bright light through the eye lids lowers the brain's levels of melatonin – the hormone responsible for causing drowsiness and inducing sleep. If you work at a job the requires doing night shifts, opt for thick curtains or a sleep mask to prevent light from entering your eyes, so that you can get the restful sleep you need.

- Use relaxation techniques to help you let go of the day's events. Whether it is just practicing deep breathing in bed, reading a book or listening to some soothing music, create a nightly ritual to signal sleep time.

Chapter 5

A Practical Guide to Managing Emotions and Overcoming Depression - Part 2: *Mental Changes*

Practice Mindfulness

Anxiety and stress can make depression worse. Fortunately, learning and regularly practicing some skills related to mindfulness, such as meditation, yoga or deep breathing, has been proven to work wonders when it comes to keeping one's emotions in check. Furthermore, some studies have shown that regularly practicing mindfulness is also effective in preventing relapse, once an individual has recovered from clinical depression.

While the benefits of mindfulness practices in regard to emotional health are extensive, there are two key factors that help relief depression. Firstly, being mindful does not change the way one feels, rather, it change the way we relate to our thoughts and feelings. So, if an individual has a tendency to feel depressed, they will learn how to avoid getting caught up in those thoughts and feelings that contribute to their sadness. Another way that mindfulness helps with depression is that, over time, sufferers learn to better tolerate and regulate their emotions.

Practicing mindfulness is simple; set aside some time everyday to mentally relax, so that you can restore a sense of calm and control in your daily life. You can take up a serious practice of meditation or yoga. If not, just doing something to aid relaxation for 15 minutes to an hour each day will suffice. Reading a few pages of a good novel, listening to soothing music, taking a long hot bath, lighting some scented candles, or enjoying a nice cup of herbal (non-caffeinated) tea to help you de-clutter you mind are all mindfulness practices.

The important thing to remember when practicing mindfulness is to focus on the present moment, and curb any negative thoughts that may bring you down.

Challenge and Silence Your Inner Critic

Ever heard the old adage that says we are our own worst enemy? All of us have an inner voice that can have a powerful and profound impact on our actions. Your inner dialog can either be constructive or destructive to your mental wellbeing. If you are unaware of what your inner voice is telling you, you may be feeding yourself lies that have accumulated over time from external suggestions. For example, those who are constantly bullied and put down by others at school can sometimes develop a tendency to formulate negative criticism of themselves. With low self-esteem comes a destructive inner dialog, such as, "I am too fat", "No one will ever love me", "I cannot succeed at anything", "No one cares about me" or "I cannot be happy".

When you inner voice frequently brings up negative affirmations, you may begin to feel a deep sense of worthlessness, hopelessness and despair. Soon, as you keep believing that inner voice, depression may sink in and you begin to persuade yourself to act out in destructive ways. To combat depression, we need to face up to our inner enemy and convert it into an ally.

Doing so involves looking critically at your past and at your current situation to determine where these critical thoughts stem from. Once you are able to do so, begin challenging the negative thoughts and feelings each time they creep up. So, let's say you feel as if you are being sidelined by your colleagues at work. Instead of allowing the feeling of isolation to bring you down, you can begin to rationalize with yourself by asking questions like "Why do I feel sad about the situation?", "What does having their attention and approval mean to me?", "Do I really need their validation and what good does it really do me?", "Does it have anything to do with my job performance?", "Is it really that bad?", "Are their criticism towards me related to my job or a petty personal attack?".

By challenging your inner voice, you will gain better clarity and understanding of situations that are affecting you emotionally. You can then consciously switch to a more positive inner dialog. Rather than berating yourself, fill your thoughts with reasoning and positive affirmations, such as, "I'll be alright", "This phase will soon come to pass", "I'm being criticized professionally, and there is no need for me to take things personally", "It's not the end of the world; I can do better next time", "Everyone makes mistakes, I'll just be more careful next time".

It is important to be compassionate and forgiving with yourself when dealing with setbacks and situations that make you feel down. Feelings of worthlessness, self-doubt and being overly critical of yourself only reinforce depression. So, along with fostering a positive inner dialog, you also want to be aware that your inner critic does not shame you by attacking how you feel during times of despair. The key is to monitor you inner dialog by not allowing the negative thoughts that make you feel low to reign free. Acknowledge those depressive thoughts, but do not believe in them.

Subdue Anger with Forgiveness

Anger is a strong emotion that often underlies and fuels depression. Although it may be a natural human emotion, it can be overwhelming and at times extremely hard to deal with. This is because we are raised and conditioned to think that anger is bad, that we must behave and not lose our temper, or else we will be punished for it. However, dealing directly with anger is necessary, so that you will not lose control and act out your feelings in harmful ways. It's possible to recognize, accept and deal with your anger in a healthy way.

Contrary to popular belief, clinical depression is not always experienced as a continuous state of painful emotions. Some suffer from depression due to suppressing feelings they are not comfortable confronting. For example, one can feel anger and resentment towards a loved one or a particular situation, but rather than acknowledging and dealing directly with how they feel, they turn those negative emotions inwards towards themselves by self-blaming and self-hatred. Worse still, an individual may also act out in abusive ways towards others, thus driving away those who care from them.

The most sensible way to release anger is by coming to terms with what it is which is causing you to feel angry, and then with a rational inner voice, gradually let go of grudges with forgiveness. Whether it's a person or a situation that is making you angry, holding on to anger is like setting off a ticking time bomb. Think about it; the source of your anger is probably unaware of how you are feeling and likely happily going about their business as usual. Is it worth allowing others to occupy your thoughts and feelings when all they are doing is bringing you down? Someone or something might have caused you grief in the past, but you have a choice in how you will react and whether or not you let them continuously affect you.

Do not think of forgiveness as admitting defeat or showing approval of those who have wronged you. Think of it instead as doing yourself a service by lightening your own emotional load, and freeing yourself from the negativity that is adversely affecting you.

Keep in Touch with a Network of

Supportive People

It can be very hard to muster up the enthusiasm to want to socialize when you are feeling depressed. In addition, emotions are contagious and the last thing you want is to be a downer to everyone around possibly leading to them eventually wanting to avoid you. Isolating yourself for some quiet time may be a good idea, but be sure to limit the time you spend alone and do your best to start getting out there again.

Social interaction is a wonderful distraction from depressing thoughts and can give a huge boost to your mood. Also, being around supportive people and enjoying activities you both have in common can help you regain a sense of purpose. It does not take much to reach out to the ones who care about you; call a friend for a catch up session, go for a walk with your partner, have lunch with family members, and if they are open to listening, talking about your depression. It feels good to have someone listen and understand what you are going through.

If you happen to move somewhere far away from your usual circle of acquaintances, get involved with the local community. Try volunteering with a local charity, join a book club, or participate in local events where you can meet new people with common interests. Nothing lifts your spirits and makes you feel less lonely than putting yourself in an active social environment. So, make an effort to get out there, even if you don't really feel like doing so. You may just meet a new friend and find a new hobby.

Explore Your Emotions Creatively

A creative endeavor – be it drawing, painting, photography, learning to play a musical instrument or simply writing a journal – is an excellent outlet which will allow you to express your thoughts and emotions. You do not have to aspire to become the next big name in art; just take up some sort of creative expression for the therapeutic benefits it is able to offer. Not only will you have a distraction from what's making you feel low, being able to produce something

creatively – and it does not have to be a masterpiece –
will give you a sense of accomplishment.

The most accessible way to express how you feel is by
keeping a journal in which you write down how you
are feeling. Try writing down what makes you feel
depressed. Then make a list of three to five things that
you are grateful for everyday; anything – no matter
how minor – that you appreciate and are grateful for.
This personal form of therapy soothes your mind in a
way that allows you to acknowledge your feelings, and
then forces you to shift towards a more positive
outlook by reminding you that things are not as bad as
they seem.

Chapter 6

A Practical Guide to Managing Emotions and Overcoming Depression - Part 3: *Must dos!*

Treat Other Underlying Causes

Having to live with a long-term medical condition that causes pain and discomfort can lead to depression. If you suffer from chronic aches and pains, work with a healthcare professional to manage and treat pain, along with your depression.

Acknowledge Your Depression and Seek Help

People suffering from depression often feel embarrassed about their condition, fearing that others will judge and think negatively and think less of them. This often leads to self-isolation, denial and reluctance to seek treatment, which does nothing but help to worsen the condition.

Know that depression is a serious mental health condition, but it is one which can be treated. However, the road to recovery must start with accepting that your mental health is out of balance, and then taking the first step towards making yourself feel better. If you find managing depression alone to be a struggle, seek help as soon as you can. Talk to loved ones about your situation and make an appointment to see a doctor. Lastly and most importantly, if you think you may harm yourself or attempt suicide, call your local emergency number or suicide prevention hotline immediately.

Never Ever Give Up on Yourself

Learning to manage and treat depression is a journey, and not an easy one. Whether you choose to go at it alone or with the guidance of a healthcare professional, you are bound to encounter setbacks along the way. Be patient and kind to yourself; take things in your stride and always try to keep an optimistic outlook, however bleak things may seem at the time. Remember that a lack of hope and belief in oneself is one of the main causes of depression. You have to do whatever it takes to stay on track with your treatment. Only by mustering up faith in yourself can you restore hope and win the battle with depression.

Chapter 7

Quick Fixes to Beat the Blues and Lift Your Mood

Making long-term changes in your life to beat depression is a gradual process. Along the way, you will encounter obstacles in your daily life that may threaten the mental equilibrium you have been working hard to cultivate. When depression triggers occur, you need to know how to prevent them from ruining your mood. Here is a list of quick fixes that you can implement immediately to beat the blues. These methods work for anyone in need of a pick-me-up; whether you are trying to overcome clinical depression or you are just going through a rough patch.

Get some sunlight

Some people suffer from a type of depression called, seasonal affective disorder (SAD), where they tend to feel low during colder times of the year when the days are shorter and the nights longer. Whether you have SAD or are just having a bad day, try to step outside when the sun is shining. You will be amazed at how the warmth of the sun can have an invigorating effect.

Pump up the beat

Listening to some upbeat music alters brain chemistry and improve mood. So, to beat the doom and gloom, put on that dance or bubblegum pop playlist for an instant change in atmosphere and channel some more positive vibes!

Laugh it all away

It may seem all too simple, but laughing can actually help convince your brain that you are happy. Whenever your critical inner voice begins to trick you into feeling bad about yourself, immerse yourself in something that will make you feel otherwise. Play your favorite comedy, binge-watch a sitcom or log on to YouTube, laugh away at funny videos, or read something funny. Turning to laughter as medicine is more than just a distraction; it is also a constant reminder that it is possible for you to feel good anytime you want.

Spend time with your pet

Your pet is really unlike other friend that you can have; they never judge you and they love you unconditionally. Playing with your pet can take your mind off of any negative feelings you are experiencing. Furthermore, caring for a pet is a fulfilling experience as you are making a commitment beyond yourself, serving as a constant reminder that you are capable of doing something worthwhile and are far from worthless.

Eat carbs

Carbohydrates raise the levels of the brain chemical, serotonin, which enhance mood and well-being. To benefit from the mood boost without packing on the pounds, be careful how much you eat. Carb-rich foods such as pasta, rice crackers, baked potato and popcorn are great options.

Indulge your sense of touch

Touch-based therapies are proven to lower levels of the stress hormone cortisol and increase the feel-good hormone oxytocin, and thus are helpful in overcoming depression. Therapies such as massage, acupressure and reflexology can work wonders in inducing relaxation and improving your mood. Having a bad day in the office? Give your masseur a call to book a session after work. You deserve it! If a massage is not available, other forms of touch will do too. Snuggle up with your significant other, get hugs from a friend (or give hugs), even cuddling with your pet or a teddy bear will have a comforting effect that can help you feel better.

Use positive self-affirmations

Remember that pesky inner critic that keeps bringing you down? Do not ever let it get the better of you. As difficult as it may be, maintaining a positive inner voice is crucial when you are feeling depressed. Whenever you sense negative talks starting up, acknowledge it and then dismiss it immediately. Counter these negative thought with positive self-affirmations. Tell yourself things like, "This will come to pass", "It's just a bad day, not a bad life", and "I'm gonna be okay, I just need a break, that's all". Again, taking a few seconds to remind yourself of all the things you have to be grateful for can be a great way of dealing with negative self talk.

Distract yourself, quickly!

It can be tempting to reach for a bottle of alcohol or pop some pills when you are feeling down. Instead of these resorting to these potentially dangerous remedies, opt for a safe distraction from feelings of depression. Call up a friend for a chat, get to that 1000 piece puzzle you have been trying to finish, or write down your feelings in a journal. Keep yourself occupied with something safe and uplifting.

Continue your treatment at all cost

Whatever depression treatment you have committed to, hang in there, have faith and stick to it. For example, if you have made a plan to journal your thoughts once every day and to attend a yoga class twice a week; keep at it and you will eventually benefit from it. There is happiness beyond depression, but you must persevere and never give up.

Get out there and don't hide away

When depression strikes, you may well feel like disappearing and isolating yourself from the rest of the world. The symptoms of depression can rob you of energy and enthusiasm, making you feel disinterested in activities you once enjoyed. Giving in to this lethargy and isolating yourself, however, is only likely to cause you to sink deeper into depression. The only way to reignite your spark and zest for life is to stay active and keep pursuing whatever it is that you enjoy. Though easier said than done, it is in the moments when you re feeling like shutting yourself off from the world that you need to force yourself to do whatever it takes to get up and do something – as much as you may feel you don't want to. Feel like moping in your room? Go out for a stroll in the park instead. Don't feel like eating? Go into the kitchen and cook up your favorite food. Too sad to drag yourself out of bed and face the day? Force yourself to get up, get dressed and step out.

At it's most basic, combating depression comes down to this: The more you learn to defy that inner negative critic, the easier it gets. Reclaim your right to be happy and do not let depression take over your life.

Conclusion

I hope this book has given you a more thorough insight into the realities of depression and the steps that you can take in order to combat the condition. Whatever the cause, understand that there is help available and that depression can be managed.

Good luck with moving forward toward a brighter future, and remember, if in doubt seek help from a trained professional.

Jane Aniston

FREE BONUS!: Preview Of

"Overcoming Anxiety - Practical Approaches You Can Use To Manage Fear & Anxiety In The Moment & Long Term"

If you enjoyed this book, I have a little bonus for you; a preview of one of my other books "Overcoming Anxiety - Practical Approaches You Can Use To Manage Fear & Anxiety In The Moment & Long Term", which goes into more detail on how you can manage anxiety safely and naturally! Enjoy!

Short excerpt from Chapter 4

Lifestyle Changes for a Long-Term Solution

Overcoming anxiety over the long haul takes more than just a few quick fixes to quell the nerves; it requires making lifestyles changes. The changes that have to be made include getting more physically active, working on achieving optimal sleep patterns, learning to handle and minimize stress better, quitting (or at least heavily cutting down on) alcohol and smoking, cutting down on caffeinated beverages, and switching to a healthier eating habit. Long-term changes cannot happen overnight; it will require commitment and patience, as you gradually take realistic steps towards improving your mental and physical health.

Get More Active

Easily the most important and helpful thing you can incorporate into your life is a regular exercise routine. Living a sedentary lifestyle filled with stress will definitely contribute to more senseless worrying. On the other hand, frequent exercise has been proven in numerous studies to reduce anxiety symptoms. Your overall well-being will benefit due to exercise causing your body to release feel-good hormones and chemicals that will improve mood and promote relaxation.

If you have never exercised regularly in the past, you can start building the habit of being more active with simple activities that get you moving. Consider taking a 30-minute stroll around the neighborhood every morning before going to work, parking your car some distance from your destination and walking the rest of the way, taking the stairs over riding the escalator, going for a nature hike on the weekends or taking a longer than usual walk with your dog. Although these may seem like relatively minor steps, if you do them regularly you'll find yourself feeling more energized and building a higher level of self discipline. This in turn should not only allow you to move on to more strenuous exercise, but is also very likely to give you a mental boost and make you feel good about yourself.

Take Up a Formal Exercise Program

To obtain the full benefit of physical activity, consider allocating time for a formal exercise program. This involves a regular set of exercises which you have to take time out of your daily life for, such as lifting weights at the gym, attending an aerobics class, or taking up a sport. It can be challenging to commit yourself to exercising, especially when you have work-life demands to fulfill. That being said, where there is a will, there is definitely a way! Think of the money spent on health club memberships and time allocated to exercising as an investment in yourself, because your well-being matters. Again, the benefits of regular excursus have been proven by numerous studies to lead to HUGE benefits; some studies have even found that exercising regularly can be as effective as taking pharmaceutical drugs when combatting conditions such as anxiety and depression!

Try Yoga

A non-religious spiritual practice that originates from India thousands of years ago, yoga has often been touted as the comprehensive mind, body and spirit workout. These claims are far from an exaggeration though. Academic research in the western world since the 1970s has considered yoga one of the best possible treatments for depression and anxiety. Since the early 2000s, yoga has gained worldwide popularity as a fitness lifestyle practice, which has lead to it becoming a staple program offered in many gyms and health clubs. There are event studios and vacation retreats dedicated to the practice, offering courses to yogis of all levels.

In a nutshell, yoga is a system of exercise that comprises deep meditation, breathing techniques and series of physical workouts in the form of postures known as *Asana*. Some of the more orthodox yoga schools and teachers would even encourage students to incorporate the spiritual (but non-religious) elements of yoga. With consistent practice, one can reap the multiple benefits of yoga, which include:

- A calm, steady and equanimous mind

- Improved mood

- Hormonal balance

- Greater flexibility and range of motion

- Greater spinal and joint health

- Improved strength and muscle tone

- Steady weight loss and maintenance

- Lowered risk of sports injury

- Lowered risk of various chronic illnesses

- Improved self-confidence

- An overall brighter outlook on life

Those who are unfamiliar with yoga may be intimidated by the demonstration of postures that seem to require a vast amount of strength and flexibility. That should not deter you from trying out this transformative workout, because there are literally hundreds of yoga postures and they vary in difficulty. Moreover, a competent instructor – known as a guru – can guide a beginner through the practice, providing modifications to difficult postures, so the student can ease themselves into the practice.

The practice of yoga has a long history, which has branched into different traditions and styles. Certain styles are more suited to relaxation, whereas some are more physically demanding. If you intend to begin practicing yoga, take time to choose a studio and teacher that offers the style of yoga best suited to your needs.

(Chapter 4 continues in the full book)

Short excerpt from Chapter 5

Cognitive Behavioral Therapy and Anxiety Disorders

Because anxiety disorders vary significantly in severity among sufferers, the treatment administered normally depends on each individual's case. One of the most common and renowned treatments for anxiety disorders is Cognitive Behavioral Therapy (CBT). It has been scientifically tested and found to be effective in hundreds of clinical trials for remedying many different mental disorders. Unlike other forms of psychotherapy, CBT is more problem-solving oriented. Patients learn specific skills that involve identifying distorted thinking patterns, modifying beliefs, relating to others differently and changing behaviors – skills which can be used for the rest of their lives.

This chapter will give you the basics on CBT, so that you will know what to expect from this treatment when seeking professional medical help for anxiety disorder.

The Theory Behind CBT

Simply put, CBT is based on the cognitive model of how the way we perceive things and situations can influence the way we feel and behave. In other words, if you interpret a situation negatively, you might feel negative emotions as a result and that in turn will lead you to behave in a certain manner. For example, someone who is obligated to attend a party might think, "This is an excellent opportunity to meet people and network!". This outlook will leave them looking forward to the event. Another person, who is less keen may think "I don't know most of the guests, so I just want to get it over and done with as quickly as possible". As you can see, it is not a situation itself that directly affects how people feel emotionally, but rather, our thoughts and perception about that situation.

When people are in distress, their perspectives and judgments are often clouded and inaccurate, causing their thoughts and imagination to run wild. CBT helps people identify thoughts that are causing them anxiety and evaluate how realistic the thoughts actually are when examined more closely. Patients then learn to change their distorted thinking patterns and adopt a more realistic approach.

(Chapter 5 continues in the full book)

Check out the rest of "Overcoming Anxiety - Practical Approaches You Can Use To Manage Fear & Anxiety In The Moment & Long Term" by me, Jane Aniston on the Amazon store!

Check Out My Other Books!

Understanding Anxiety *- Why You're Suffering From Anxiety & How You Can Start Breaking Free!*

Overcoming Anxiety *-Practical Approaches You Can Use To Manage Fear & Anxiety In The Moment & Long Term*

Depression - Practical & Natural Approaches You Can Use To Cure Depression In The Moment & Long Term

Cognitive Behavioral Therapy - A Practical Guide To C.B.T. For Overcoming Anxiety, Depression, Addictions & Other Psychological Conditions

Homemade Shampoo (Includes 34 Organic Shampoo Recipes!)

Homemade Makeup (Includes 28 Organic Makeup Recipes!)

Homemade Deodorant (Includes 20 Organic Deodorant Recipes!)

Homemade Lip Balm (Includes 22 Organic Lip Balm Recipes!)

Homemade Bath Salts (Includes 35 Organic Bath Salt Recipes!)

(All books available as digital downloads and printed books)